Alhambra Geometric
Pattern Coloring Book

Featuring a selection of 30 geometric pattern coloring pages, this book is suitable for adults and children. Guaranteed to give you relaxation and creativity during your coloring.

The pages are single sided to prevent bleed through the paper and covered with a black page to make it even better.

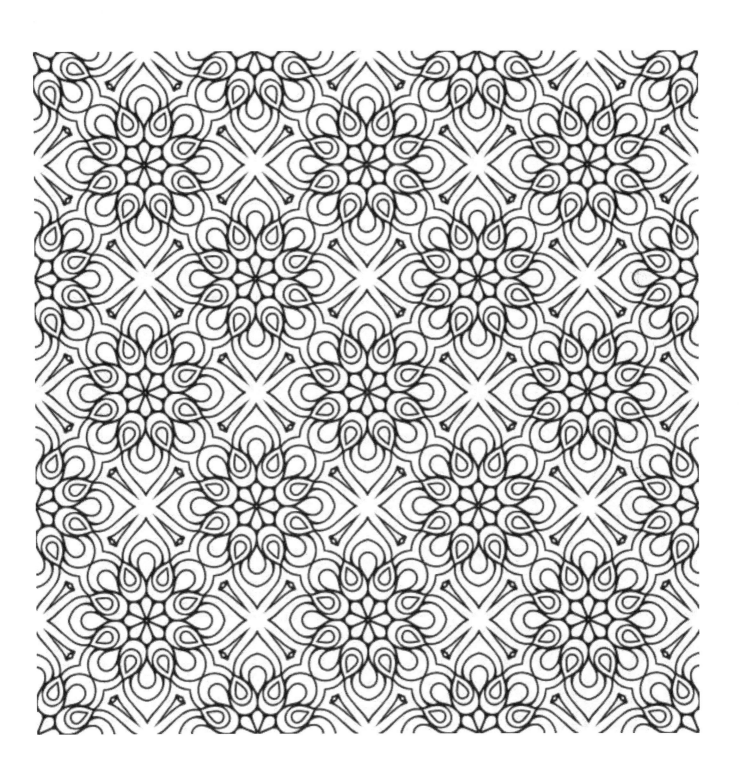

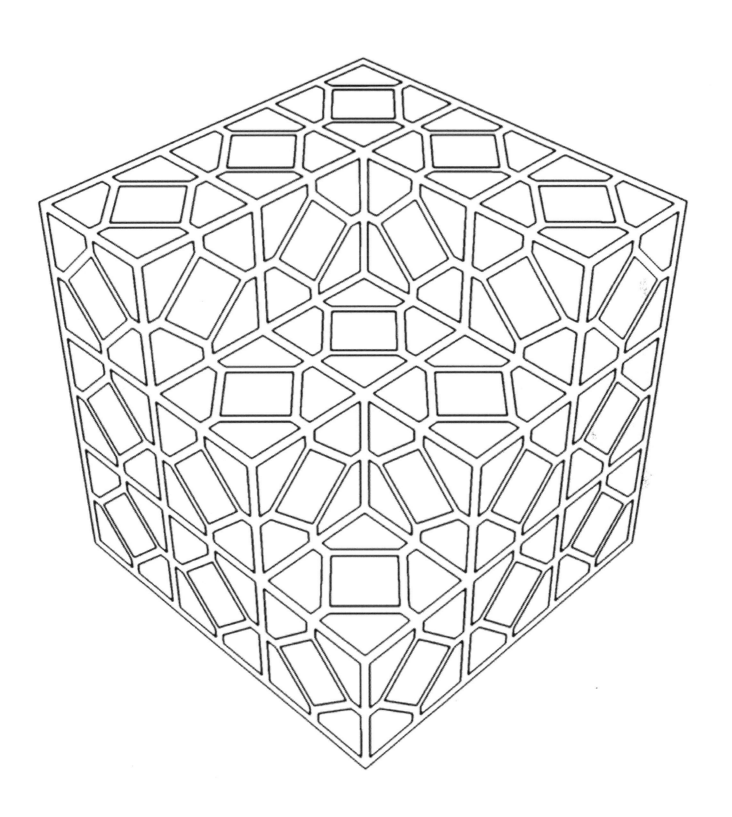

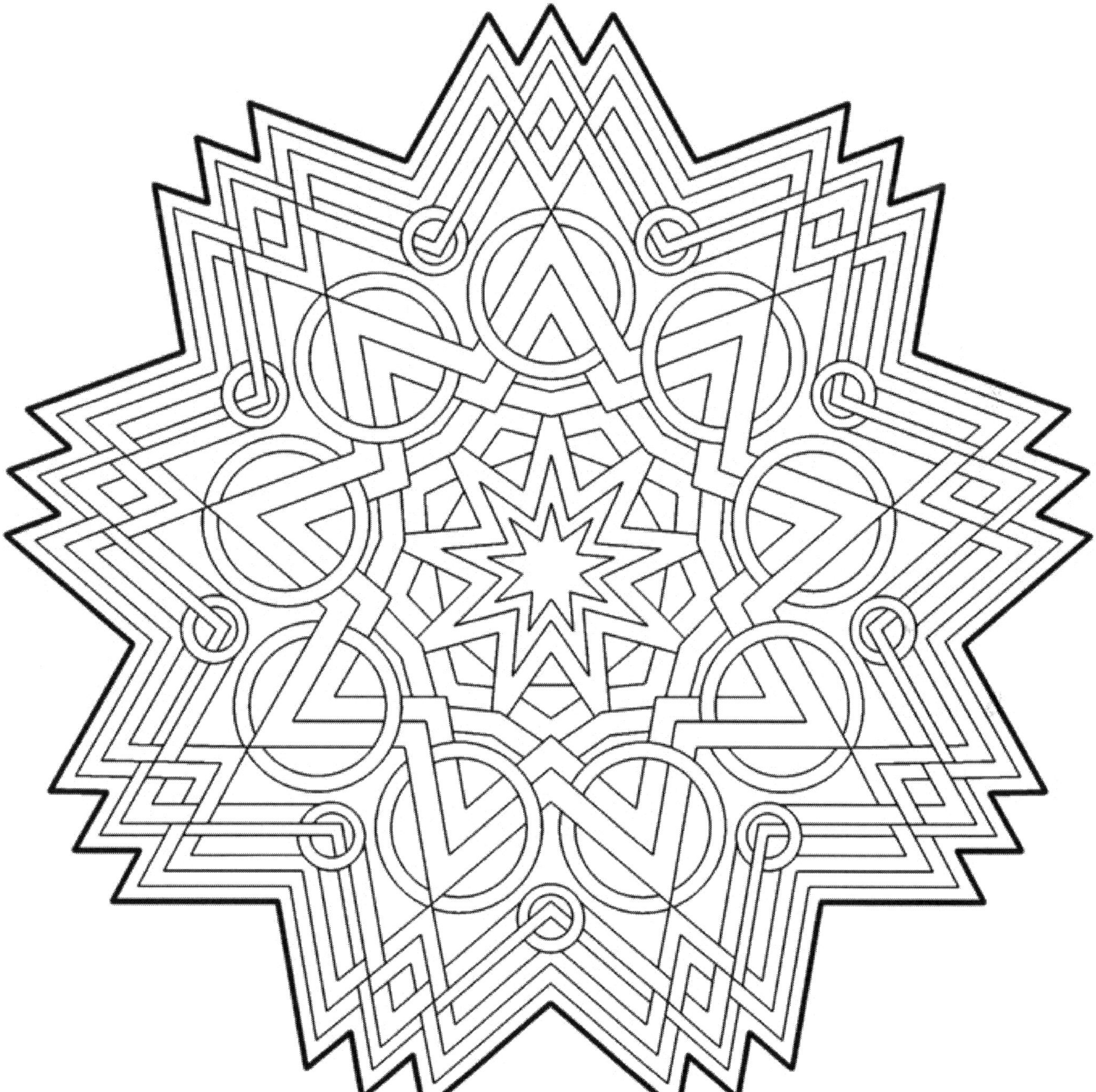

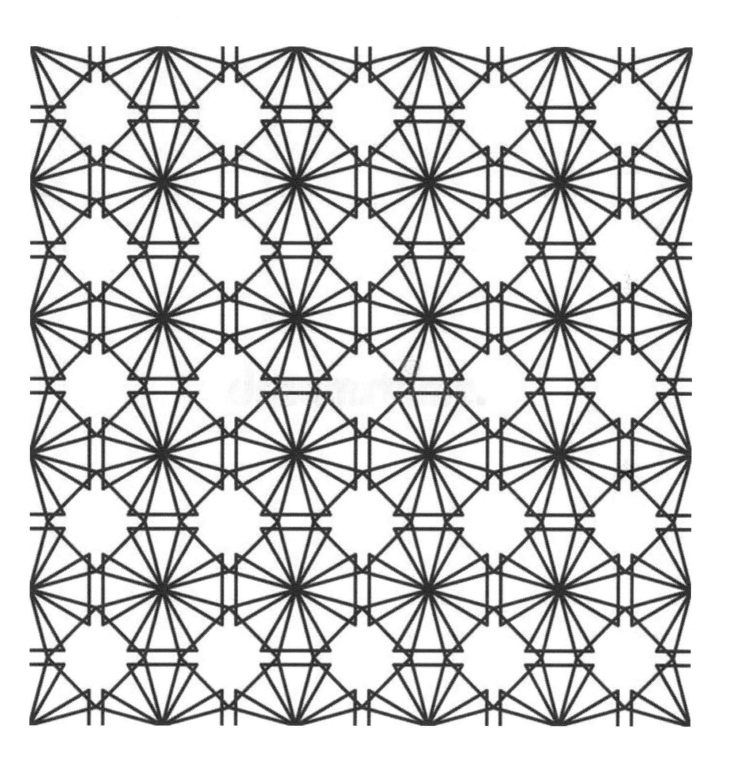

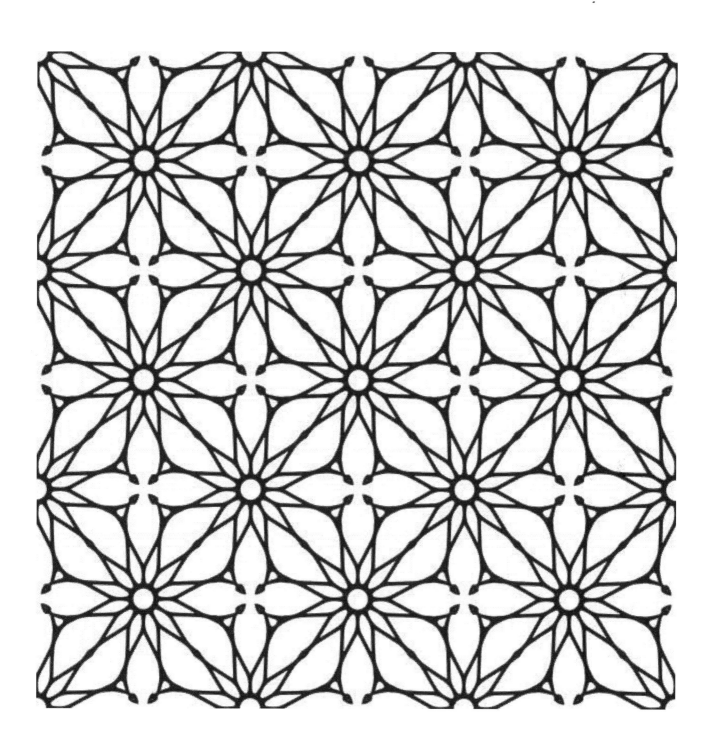

Made in United States
Troutdale, OR
06/13/2024